PLAY | HOUSE

PLAY | HOUSE

POEMS

JORRELL WATKINS

CURBSTONE BOOKS / NORTHWESTERN UNIVERSITY PRESS
EVANSTON, ILLINOIS

Curbstone Books

Northwestern University Press

www.nupress.northwestern.edu

Copyright © 2024 by Jorrell Watkins. Published 2024 by Curbstone Books / Northwestern

University Press. All rights reserved.

Printed in the United States of America

10 9 8 7 6 5 4 3 2 1

LIBRARY OF CONGRESS CATALOGING-IN-PUBLICATION DATA

Names: Watkins, Jorrell, author.

Title: PlayHouse : poems / Jorrell Watkins.

Other titles: Play house

Description: Evanston, Illinois : Curbstone Books/Northwestern University Press, 2024.

Identifiers: LCCN 2023043452 | ISBN 9780810147133 (paperback) | ISBN 9780810147140 (ebook)

Subjects: LCSH: African American men—Poetry. | LCGFT: Poetry.

Classification: LCC PS3623.A869444 P53 2024 | DDC 811.6—dc23

LC record available at https://lccn.loc.gov/2023043452

For my brothers, Joseph, Colbey, and Malachai

I can't blame white people for not feeling
the rhythm like black people, especially when it comes
to jazz and blues because it took many lives
to make this kind of music.

—EDDIE BOYD

CONTENTS

HOUSE BELOW THE HEAVENS

Brotha Speaks | 3

IEP | 5

Hustle Hard | 6

Cut the Grass | 8

Up a Notch | 10

Acquisition: Mothership | 11

Toyhouse | 12

Sleepover at Richard's: Backyard | 13

Of the White Tee | 15

Acquisition: Boombox Carried by Radio Raheem | 17

Cop a | 18

His Bounty | 19

Nine Mile Road | 20

Sunday before Last | 22

Hymn | 23

HALFWAY BLUES HOUSE

Ah Bae: Blues Haibun | 27

Acquisition: Coltrane's Saxophone | 28

Sugar | 29

Honey | 30

Iced | 32

Tea | 33

Acquisition: Dress from *Lady Sings the Blues* | 34

Snowfall with Ruth Brown's *Bringdown* | 35

Mean what I say | 36

A Drive through July Showers | 37

Day, Dawn & Dusk Mess with My Blues | 39

4:04 A.M. | 41

Today Got Me | 43

Yesterday | 44

Apple Pie | 45

Nah-Nah: Trap Haibun | 47

TRAPHOUSE

In the House | 51

Oh brother, where did all the bullets go | 52

Anotha Brotha | 54

Would | 56

When a Tree Falls | 58

After April 11, 2021 | 59

Witness | 60

Blicky | 61

wat dey do | 63

Bando Ballade | 64

Grey Gah | 66

Notes on Kumite | 67

Payback Gets Played Back | 70

Acquisition: Coded Language Scroll | 72

Ah-man | 73

Brotha Moves | 75

When I go | 77

Notes   79

Acknowledgments   83

HOUSE BELOW THE HEAVENS

Brotha Speaks

Eggs sizzling in the pan Mama taught me at five
my eyes met the stove eyes twisted dial to warm
bathtub foam mustache she rubbing oil on hives

eczema and asthma take after flowers with thorn
berries from pokeweed dyed me inexcusable red
nicknamed tone of sunbeam, monotonous mourn

kids around-the-way left their hurt widespread
bruises my fleshroux simmered best in autumn
back-to-school season in hand-me-down threads

those boys who didn't look like me, fought them
until they looked like me, scraps from poplar bark
ah bae, all day my belly pangs wanted to blossom

sheetrock—punch threw, my knuckles worn darts
across the room Mama *nah-nah*, I'm not like Pops
got nothing to swallow, smacked gums like shark

grey gah, mouth spat gutta, maggot brain slop
brotha wanted out, brobro block posse hanging
slinging sludge the grind of grime, manhole ops

open carry Texas Instruments dumbstruck banging
Fiasco over Badazz my brah trapped ganggang vine
rap persona snowman *ah man*, brobro you slanging

*

3

His guise jail cell dim resembles psych ward shine
immolate soul childhood ashes collude his pupils
future snapped, smushed forty on his twenty-nine

losing matter, scarecrow exo, lunch convo fruitful
saying something with color, just a pinch of music
nodding, can't prod, blood abides by some scruples

we sated I reach for affection, he Jackson *don't do it*
there's only air between us, I ask him basic math—
I know I aint right, he mutters Daddy's cuss, I lose it

air between us flares from Cain-inherited wrath
his chest, paper-mache I clench, *nigga watch yo filth*
disgust blew me astray, distrust corroded our pact

*

I'll play songs for you, something you can get with
we don't have to talk, let music restore what we built

IEP

Play Lupe Fiasco's "Paris, Tokyo"

My brother and I attend
A. Hill Middle School.
Two years senior, grade ahead,
he's always booked hallways
above. Through crevice where
flights of stairs spiral dim
I look up, *it's him*;
at least once, unscheduled,
I see him leaving detention-P.E.,
we nod. Third-floor guideposts
prohibit his speech. He doesn't face
Japanese or French, knows
there's another language
I'm grasping, his want.
His plan doesn't take him
to Japan, France, courses
reserved *advance.* I motion,
come down that hill; mouth
join me side by side. School bells
and there he goes without

Hustle Hard

for my boys Kite, Jeezy, and Kilo

Eight blocks
from my mama's house,
intersection of Belmont and Grant,
I trudge:
       snapped wooden rake
       electric weed whacker
       gas-powered handheld leaf blower
all on top of lawn mower.

Here I am:
       grass stains smeared on ashy Wrangler jeans
       bleach dots less noticeable than grease spots
       that cling to mesh of my oversized jersey
       like the clump of moist grass underneath
                     a lawn mower's blade

I study the block:
every knob, doorbell
smudged with oil-sweat.

I zigzag-mow backyards, tote
lawn & leaf bags like some August
Christmas sack, curb–alley.

Splintered fingers, dusty kicks
I submit to evening's blaze only
after a brotha gets paid.

Downbottom boys claim,
only grass worth cutting on scale.

My cabbage leaves can't compare
to rosebush thickets growing
from out their pockets.

Them boys run everything nonstop;
couple ells embellish their lips
selling loud, wielding heat
designer jeans define their being.

Them boys bang harder than a stone
caught in the whirl   of a lawn mower's blade.

Somewhere beyond Belmont and Grant,
I cut grass-dirt.

Cut the Grass

for my father

When you are standing
over the mower sweat sizzling
in grease and sludge coalesced
by evening sun as she,
with teeth brimming, hands you a rag
will you have cut the grass.

When you apply WD-40
to blades, pour gasoline down
pipe, and yank machine
to life, she'll tell you
that you are hers and she
is yours.

When the grass no longer
dances in the wind
crickets leap over anthills
roots sprawl about like thoughts
of marriage and family
spring will come.

If you want to be loved
as blades of steel colliding
with blades of grass, you must
cut the grass.

Cut the grass until crickets believe
they are flying when they leap.
Cut the grass and release
the pheromones of combusted oil.

Cut the grass and see fertile dirt
that wants to nurture your seed.

If you don't:
> The mower will rust under
> the fall of summer's rain.
> Thoughts of lost family
> will winter your soil.
> She'll hold the rag
> in her hands.
> The grass between you
> will grow dense as teeth.

Up a Notch

Jody and I watch *Emeril Live*.
Today, he cooks Cajun cuisine.
We stick-sofa, legs pretzeled,
backs starched. Emeril pinches
rock salt, shimmering broth,
tosses minced garlic, chopped onions,
celery, bell peppers—*Bam!*
Creole seasonings. [*commercial break*]
We gut Mama's spice cabinet:
cayenne, paprika, garlic powder,
oregano, basil, and thyme. Repurpose
Fold & Close sandwich bags,
gourmet flasks—[*Emeril's back*].
The Gulf of Mexico floats in
Emeril's cast-iron pot. A dirty rice–
filled skillet schemes across
Emeril's island. We whet violence;
the ground innards of American hog,
lobster claw shot from its broth bath—
Bam! Secret ingredient [*break*],
Jody shakes Louisiana Hot, I Texas Pete.
Concoctions made, teaspoons drawn,
which taste bombards the palate?
Jody's nose bleeds, my throat peels.
[*again*] Emeril's jazz band muses
his Cajun creation. Jody froths chili-mucus,
I hack heavy metal. Mama finds us shrunk
fetal on her kitchen tile—*Bam!*
Paper towel, 2%. [*TV goes off*]
Mama cooks comfort.

Acquisition: Mothership

Dazzle Mama, come! Beam from slumber
Tune us maroon, capsule the captor's dim
Imbibe atmospheric sprite, constellation's spawn
We fauna no longer, code *Black*, virtual route
Transcending our trendsetting, conscious slay

Under the groove our steps collate minds
Maggot brain culture we kilowatt the bots
Overcharged, bail out systematic headlock
Bypass the rulers, circuit trip this business
One hundred and fifteen claps per minute

Planet hertz children disrupt rhythm and funk
Mother Earth cooling, we got a way with waves
Words mean something cousin, blow soul
Equip solar panel goggles, we creating current
Flow fold the world within our celestial rap

Toyhouse

Jody and I are princes inside.
There's no T-Rex drawing
his fangs around our queen.
Meat-eating dinosaurs aren't
quartered at all. Blue and Black
Rangers brawl day, dawn and dusk.
Dark Magicians flicker wands,
spell-bound Beyblades twist
Teflon-brass. No one has to share
a bed. Lego work crew blocks
room for guests. Outside there's
train for regional transit. We sit
on tracks, get up right as train
loops back. Camaro, Thunderbird,
Eclipse: the model cars our king
built. We don't touch 'em, decal
our reflection onto plastic. Jody
thinks G.I. Joe left gadgets to
fill his absence. I say,
He's on mission to keep reptiles away.
We don't see Joe or Rex for months.
Our queen slumps floral sofa, TV
turned Joel Osteen, King of Kings'
book, breathing mask on her face.
I would ask for her opinion; I can
no longer tell when she's sleeping.

Sleepover at Richard's: Backyard

Pollen coats everything

Uncared for—my sleeveless arms yolk,

My brother,

Joseph kernel. I believe sun

Must watch and wood hold sound; what wills

Voice?

One end of yard, pit barks,

Sloshes saliva settles amalgam. Front of us,

Rich;

Holding his BB gun: orange nozzle

Pried off, jet black, absent light. His humor:

Rich fires

Shells at our feet. Our knock-off

Kicks gush-melted plastic, crush ant-

Hills beneath.

His aim compacts: chest, gut, shin.

Joseph hoists his Faded Glory,

No avail he faints.

I'm stuck, unlearning movement,

I still until pellets flip me—out of footing,

Outward light.

Did sun just blink?

Magnolia soaks in audible: golden I splay,

Pit licking its silver, Rich reloads, my brother

Unhusked as dirt.

Of the White Tee

bruh, aint a new
white tee the most
necessary dress to boom
a Black boy's joy? don't he

look so fresh
and clean, his white tee
nearly kisses his knees, veiled
by his name-brand jeans which
saddle the heels of his air force ones.

aint this gown
for him to stroll down the block:
        pass shorties rocking hoops
round their hips and ears,
        pass homies fixing a jay
and the laces of their jays,
        pass junkies sucking
blues from a bottle or needle dry.

won't them folks
dazzled by his gleam
        yo!
don't he almost glow
into an angel before
a sole streetlight
shines a halo out
of the basketball rim—

under which other
white tees will join him
in tossing the rock   once swung
        between the archway of someone's legs
then flung from half-court
by a tee, who's too short
to play center but has a jumper
that makes the whole
backboard thunder—

don't their birds' chests swell
for a moment of breathlessness
        feeling free in their white tees from
the description that matches them all

        these boys flock away as doves
at the burst of noise that sounds
like anything but their joy.

Acquisition: Boombox Carried by Radio Raheem

Tecsonic Promax Super Jumbo Boom
BedStuy rock Brooklyn swing Harlem Queens

Fight the Power we the people call 'em
Public Enemy same bop looped nonstop
Malcolm and Martin smiling two bucks please

Turn it up shaved ice soak music it's syrup
kids enjoy it hawt day take five gon' tend
some business spend this sweat blasting sense

Errbody incense tune We Love Radio—
Raheem "blasting that big box, cold rocking the scene"

Mayor can't hold peace people let loose
Buggin' Out hollerin' haints bluebodies
Soiled napkins hosed tanktops spaghetti straps

Billy sticks—chants rumble Mother Sister wails
Blast that big box, cold rotting the sheen.

Cop a

after Nas

Dad, we moved away from the strays
a glint against our glass means moon.
No need for pitbull, we got ADT
gorgeous cypress fence and tinted trucks.
Each day we drive to work we do
return. Stomach supper, the evening news.

If God gives me tomorrow, pray I don't cop a—

'01 gold Chevy Impala, me shotgun
big bro driving, Baptist-ABC-lot passin'
we choppin' it up, bro putting me on blast
sixteen living ways, six–ten minimum wage
that's better than stacking at Southside Plaza
some jokers have a problem *stick it* through your
window, barrel sockets wasteland your wallet
smarter now tellin me "check the glove compartment."

If God gives me tomorrow, pray I don't cop a—

Done walked across two stages, done talked
in front of too many rooms, won't I role model
material? Your twenty-first, first thing you do
roll down Midlothian to Colonial, come back
with Jack Daniels, Smith & Wesson. Saying
you got friends in higher places, why brother?

If God gives me tomorrow, pray I don't cop a—

18

His Bounty

He claims he's going to put Colorado
out of business by end of summer.
His homegrown started humble, bud in red
Solo cup propped against sunlit glass.
One thunderstorm away
from being seen above our fence.

He thinks the FBI tracks his supply;
eight o'clock he harvests evidence
in Royal Dansk tin still noisy
with crumbs since '08 Christmas.

Dusk he pries lid, takes whiff
of Virginia funk, fixes spliff and flicks
Music Choice channel from "Ruff Ryders'
Anthem" to "Heaven Sent"

He's faded at last
his spoken chicken-scratch coughs
soothed snores, oscillate ripples
in his Coca-Cola glass.

It's almost August and all his
product sits on kitchen table:
we eat our meals, drop off our keys,
and believe what's left is plenty.

Nine Mile Road

for Tyrell and Vadon

Every Friday Ty,
'Don, and I nightcruise
other side of town, run-
down Fairfield Mall dust dull
background soaking cookout yellow
glow trimmed artery red lit sign,
It's Bo Time. Quarter-ten we pull in,
greet cashiers with names
we dance to say, *what's your order?*

For some reason, our chins tilt,
glares pan every item, each person—
we searching their menu as if it knew
we buy Bojangles: 8pc chicken
4pc biscuits box, three
water cups or (depending on
who treating or who check us out)
one half-gallon
tongue smack iced tea.

Couple nail clinks intercoms our meal,
we the only guests in here yet. 'Don
finds our booth, Ty snatches napkin
after napkin he knows I hate asking
in how I keep saying, *forgot to ask,*
even how habitual this may seem
we never think *utensils, plates, prayer?*
we sink our blunt-want in white-dark *here,*
we drain our hot-want with white/dark *clear.*

This comfort:
My arm cross 'Don's arm
his hand Ty's hand grazes
my thumb on 'Don's knuckle
his wrist sheens slick Ty's
fingertips rub oil, butter
another warm thing palmed
pulled closer warm want and I
can't trace whose want goes where.

In separate homes with familiar creed
our mamas raised us Black and shame-free
she sacrificed to make our living mean
which means and has meant she didn't
let no one go hungry even if she had to
yet over here, us trio, string nocturnes
in my 260K-mile'd lemon burn Nine Mile Rd.
for hunger our mamas know will be
our demise if not shone as boyish delight.

The chicken aint all that bad
we clean bone, leave no mistake
save our doppelganger maroon cushion
slow-goes-it inflates plush as we rise up
well after close, we fold in and light rolls
this side of town into the next.
We surrender to night's demands,
having staved off our want
without ever coming close to full.

Sunday before Last

Scenting air, sense atmosphere: powder-creamed decaf
and bacon fat, Gma praise-crowned & worship-gowned from service picks
beefsteak tomatoes, too rare to spoil outside, Frigidaire is carved and Pops
maws hardwood-smoked Gwaltney; its excess gilding Merita white. He flops cognac
chair, fastens sweat leather. Dandruff ashens his crown, aftermath of Wahl clippers
and mosquito heat milling about his scalp.   Six decades and bulging veins still bull
tendons, muscle—settle this month's debts. My veins flush their blood, slight of coursing
half the laps of Pops—fourth of Gma's; how will I someday guide their arks to bank?
Coming through, Pops drags a jay on way to room-which-never-gets-used. Vinyl
unsheathed and set, "International Lover" cajoles every nook of house—we move:
Gma–prayer, myself–chores, Pops croons his yearnings, hollow all over the world
as he slides each arm into his everyday work jacket.

Hymn

for Joseph

       No one named Joseph wants to be
called such.
       Joseph resounds title, gauge
consequence:
       Guardian, husband, father.
My brother
       Inherited his name from our father;
as did our papa.
       Our makers require us: instruction
in given name,
       Obligation in family. Appraise love,
is labor. The firstborn
       Accrues debt from their making.
Anybody after
       (If there is an after) whelms them
further in curse.
       I, with the strain of cuss, say,
Joseph.
       My brother won't hold
Papa's filth.
       Why he lifts to noise
scored by his throe,
                  I can't bear.

HALFWAY BLUES HOUSE

Ah Bae: Blues Haibun

I don't wanna tell a story, especially one that has already been told practically worn out from the different mouths it was summoned from, then bellowed. I don't wanna tell a story . . . came here looking for something. I don't know what it looks like. A partner of mine might say, "It is, what you aint." I don't wanna sell a story. No good at keeping promises, good at wandering on others' premises—*Oh this your home? My bad, wrong door.* Sure glad there aint a shotgun propped against the wall.

alcove window fog reads the walk: lighthouse glint

Look different today, that I do. Left the market brand funkin' new. Right away picked up a "check you out!" Did a turn-around in the middle of the boulevard. Look different today, that I do! Crisscross Stacy Adams on curb stop, tootsie roll my thighs, knee high socks showin', slacks cuffs climbin', I'm spookin' out the corner of they guise. Look different today— that I don't, against the wall or on the ground.

freezing rain   asphalt still as fault presses black ice

Hush . . . ah bae think a train's coming. It's running electric. That gotta be fast that gotta be that gottagotta—you know, our pulse is electric? Aint talking about no static there's a dynamic circuit in us bae. If you take this hand, my rails and your rails could make station out of prairie. Hush . . . ah bae think a train's coming. Got your ticket? Got your wallet? Got your— what you mean you aint going. Why you running so fast? That ottaotta day you know you pause . . . aint talking about no stagger, there were surges in us bae. You took this hand, my ails and your ails, mistakes and all prayers we whispered. Us . . . all day . . . us all—bae. Think a train's coming . . . gonna go lay my head. Against the wall, or on the ground. Right where you can see it.

soft cold mist, close the curtain—   drenched skull and nape

Acquisition: Coltrane's Saxophone

Air, the color of *Blue World*,
siphoned from blimp-sized lungs
propels like train with nowhere
to return, through the mouthpiece
committed to Coltrane's lips
bound by ligature, gold lantern
at tunnel's entrance, inside
its curled neck muses cold depth
boxed and compressed
by valves: notes scaling
atmosphere, circulates bow
as body heaves from successive
hooks, arrives as steam at bell.
Coltrane blows again,
blues deluge globe in dearth.

Sugar

I fall for everything with pulse:
some dog licking its tail, its owner
on the sidewalk slab we share
not speaking or thinking
about the underneath which moves even
when we settle. For anything
with teeth I'll surrender
rake my account of coin
off ring—on sight—moment of.

There was a word for this
I swallowed it
forgot its shape and music.
I've lost touch and sound mind.
I keep putting hands in pockets
and wonder why everything I touch dries.

I gotta stop acting
like I aint never did nothing.
Somebody rattled me
to their rhythm, spun me in
just took me in, in—
rush me in and—
gave and gave and—sweet Jesus

I aint never done nothing

Fall into something greater
dissolve in the awe of being in,
losing and gaining
everything.

Honey

I saw stranger.
Looked again, saw friend.
Saw small town
only locals know
how to pronounce. Friend,

Still there looking for you.
I ought to give you a ring.
I dial numbers I know by heart.
Still haven't set up your voicemail
      I see.
You ring commencement bell.
Everyone cheers.
Our five-dollar Moscato
ferments more. Vanilla frosting
gleams the cake. I can't hold
cheer, wine, cake—you.

My laugh is *You living Hollywood*,
I'm living the Woods—not the woods
where I storm out of your place onto a strip
of vivids that could rob me of liquid—
woods where I follow your promise
of farm-made ice cream, apple picking.
Lactose intolerant, I swallow
this honeycrisp. This harvest
I'm one shy mouth from finishing

I'm one month shy from finishing
hardest thirty-day recovery.

Therapist I won't listen.
I ring everyone, *yeah, it gets better.*
Yeah, at being worse.

I thirst for sparkling water
and milk that isn't milk.
I purchase spinach prewashed
in plastic—
            Who the hell am I becoming?
I see stranger. Look again,
I see your grin. On mannequins,
Calvin Klein you say I'd look good in.
Bought shop. Left window.
My credit's depressed.
I send postcards to each address I discover.

People call me mister now.
I mistook you for somebody
I shouldn't. I almost gave them
a ring. I'm repeating everything
            I said, must stop.

Iced

Rink's edge I glare depth in bestowed rings
etched by darlings scarf-discarded, unbound
by how fleeting everything savored will turn.
Their skates cut frolic evidence. I urn
its shavings, stack myself powder metropolis:
skyscrapers, towers, business outside this park.
Workers hurtle elements toward shelter
wearing rubber, metal, leather, plastic layers,
whirring public transit, inaudible as snow—
turns moisture on my varnished nose and cheeks.
Those fools hook bare hands, cleave liminal
space unruly. They're swift-kissing the mist,
twisting duty and risk out of sight, thought.
Out there serving royalty, subjects of none.

Tea

What is it
that melts layers
despite the gargle
of wintry mix
we steep
midday
between shifts,
lunch hour traffic,
happenstance
of our intersecting commutes?

What feeling diffuses us
makes domestic disaster
of soak and filth, honeys
the funk consumed . . .

soul trough settle, close
yourself light, surrender
to dim our two selves
are tethered. Find words,
spoon breath. Fulgurate microphone,
podium from units of me—
you need. I'll feedback

monitor, solar plexus, blur
our static stir-ring. Oneness,
whir-ring itself, this room
blurts-pulse. Pushes door ajar,
pulls wide nightstand's drawer;
where your studs vanish
beside my favorite frames.

Acquisition: Dress from *Lady Sings the Blues*

Queen of Motown flourish in cream blue,
fur-trimmed jacket buttoned over floor-
      length teal. Regal, fleeting luster gardenia cleave
Diana from fracture Billie sing blues no other
      voice can swallow river and mud, make bank
out of channel, her rasp: air scuttling surface—
      water, wine, lager, liquor—café Manhattan murmur
Society. Lady Day sop up grime, ism-venom, cut
      albums, plume of Dixie fowl, strange pome
nibble on it, gut swashes decades after Jessie,
      'fore Emmett, on mic bleached in glamour glitz—
excess hacks Holiday into daze: week in prison,
      stint at Carnegie. Applause dulls the songs that
gnaw inside-out. May Diana remove Billie's blues,
      its sediment drifts wherever the current unsettles.

Snowfall with Ruth Brown's *Bringdown*

Twenty–degree snow. Cloud whisper,
I feel–hear. Stark bleak trinkets crinkle

a little chime, *Mercy my darling I can't*
bear the fall. The distance grows, winter

outlasts us all. Shovel and scraper work against
bringdown. Damp dim I'm digging–undo—

Cold refuse, mud glacier wavering—passing howl.
All around still, my soul stirs I turn–plow

and pile the sounds plunging from above. I faint in
what fades. 'Down lighter, blaze slow troublesome hum.

Mean what I say

There's three-fourths gallon of pecan streusel bread
pudding on second shelf right door garage fridge.
Don't know if nuts are too much, but it's from
brotha-owned shop cross town. Asked baker's clerk,
Are we living each moment's worth? Was no need
to explain that one side of town is dazed from
midnight-blue sedan that sped the red of Hazelhurst
and Brook as lightning shook this city dark. And yes,
there's itch of an unmarked Crown Vic that noticed
waxing flurry underneath waning vroom. Telling you,
as said before, my doom is coming no faster than this
slow living I'm after; *our time's worthy.* Come now
bae, here is our sustenance; indulge us serving.

A Drive through July Showers

Have you ever stopped at a light
and hoped it didn't turn green?

That your car would soak the velvet
luminescence and become the lover
that sponged passion from your touch?

Have you ever touched something
and felt it withdraw? Like a poorly
aligned steering wheel veering
far from the right—

Would you feel right if tailgate
passes you in speed-up rage
while you abide by cautious eyes
ensuring the safety of those around you?

Would you feel safe under scalding rain
that croons about love to die for?
Might you think to twist dial and
seek a beat that will soothe you.

Maybe you'll study windshield wipers
in idleness and stir about a sway
unlike splattered raindrops, smeared
lipstick stains hazy imprint—

It looks just like the rosy mist of
stoplight radiance striking vapor
risen from running car's hood.

If this light turns green how would
you know when to stop moving on?

Day, Dawn & Dusk Mess with My Blues

Don't swing my melody
each bar grafted from melancholy
bulge, too troublesome.

Song don't need uplifting
                some people do.

Look about the crowds and count
                the crowns.
        Single out few whose jewels
are still lustrous
                as their lover's silk.
They still nauseous from the must
                of the last fabric they clutched after—
who knows what happened . . .

My melody is me
        not no turn-it-on, sing-along nonsense
        to feed people's jubilating feet.

                No sir, I gorge song
                for rock bottoms—mood
                heavy blue
                it levels the room
                fits my lopsided stool.

Seems swing is all you bring
don't intrude this balance.
        If my melody tugs somebody

to lean against wall,
let that body slump itself,
stone buttress.
Come Day, Dawn & Dusk,
there aint no swinging that.

4:04 A.M.

(The YouTube algorithm plays Day, Dawn & Dusk's rendition of "Sleep Kentucky Babe" after Quavo of Migos complains Offset talks too loud on the phone and Takeoff, thinking of the success of the "Walk It Talk It" music video, pens ideas for a lullabye.)

Skeezers (nah-nah) hear my honey's subtle vibe
Kentucky bae, sleep, sleep fly away (gone)

Sandman coming—*here*, R.I.P. the child in me
Kentucky bae (ah bae), sleep, sleep fly away

Silkmoon dripdrip glimmers the chandelier flair
bezel bling (beam) putting on the latest glo
ol' Kentucky might just lose your lime' tonight

Close them eyes and sleep
fly away, fly away,
my Kentucky bae

Fly away, fly away,
my Kentucky bae

Fly away, fly away,
my Kentucky bae

*

Bare dawn and celestial shine
intrudes our room. I see moon
melt and cool, loud fumes lift me
skyside, wraith-like draped *other life*.
I'm enthralled: cosmic chaos
brimming sacrificial light. I want
bright beings to end me
with lightspeed, matter me sound:
a vibe viable in dense blue-black
liminal spaces.

Bae, our walls pulse
because of us. Your sleep starts
after we rip apart. I'd join you tho—
The stars are calling for me

Today Got Me

sweating worry
        on my pillow cover
drawn curtains drain morning
        mattress soaks trouble
I might drown in hebetude
        without splatter
blues slips in my pores
        what can I do
with pockets dry as chalk
        and scribble-scrabble doubts
today weighs me terrible
        wanna slumber into yesterday
before I even had thought
        of what today got me

Yesterday

Tasted dank.
Slurped, dripped
sloshed under.

Stood, sank. Felt
deep take, shade
ablution. Evening

nocturnes flushed.
Wail everywhere's
crypt. Harrowing

silence know sol;
belie. *Alive,* uncertain
condition depends—

who's looking?
Great trouble, toggle:
neighbor, vigilant.

Pursue dilemma
Streetlight–streetlight;
watchtowers. Shelter

off-kilter, dim
drawn vagabond
no land's vault.

Apple Pie

A young white lad looks
out of the corner of his eye sees between
the slit of stitched-cloth seat cushions a
slice of apple pie riding the train
with no one for company except a black
manye by the name of George, yeah.

His name must be George, yeah.
"Nigger" would suffice but he look
too clean with his cap and black
tie on white shirt and handkerchief between
sport coat's pocket and chest. On the train
he is George. He is not Curtis, a

black man escaping the Delta, or a
Thomas who loves to swoon young doves, yeah.
He wised up from Marvin who'd crooned each train
as his place to reign. Though sometimes he look
like Leonard raising a slim between
his fingers, the ashes falling like the burnt black

stiff cut from the tip of scorched black
rope clung to the throat of a
jocular coon who peaked between
the thighs of a southern white belle, yeah.
This brotha knows better, he gotta look
like George, the Pullman porter of every train.

Leave home in Virginia for a bunk on the train.
His dreams droop and his lips black

and swell hopelessness as he look
but doesn't stare for he gotta be a
yessir, yes ma'am, servicing Negro, yeah.
His only chance for escape lies between

11 P.M. and 5 A.M., possibly at brothel between
Ray's gambling house and not his town's train
station or cemetery-buried auction block, yeah.
His corner, the reserved wedge of black
space among Pullman's sleeping cars, is a
repaired roof over well-fed kids. Although he look

mighty famished between the lad who look
like he's gonna burst on this train to save a
slice of pie, yeah. Apple pie threatened by black.

Nah-Nah: Trap Haibun

In vile funk, Vaseline shudders. Got trouble, dem boys watching; dey
quota not gonna bonus dem cross country. Holiday here, got tickets.
Parking meter? I aint see it. Fine, charge, execute. Not permanent but
damages huh? Guilty until proven incompetent, sick with this. Sic
mastiff, guarantee me stiff. Guaranteed life insurance, ninety-eight dollars
a month, four weeks behind on payment, two-dollar interest got me
tripping. Brake on busy-busy—what the name of this street? Aint it after
five? *I'm not fin, I'm not finna*—huh? Pop the trunk? nah-nah, I'm just out
to get some—

      Air;   horns blare for gold, glowing between emerald and ruby

Took tooth to clench my crown. Yo mans aint riding shotty. nah-nah,
We Cadillac DeVille: seats nimbus, Black Ice Tree necklace, hood:king
mattress, chrome got charm, rims got ribs, car cleaner than cane. Slick as
dap-clasped Jackson. Clip got foliage. We eating . . . evening turn morning
when my locomotive come humming.

          *

                             Coming home, the sky squints.
Chopper hovers from the corner of a building; don't got any business
with—Five below. Five above. Limit: 25 residential. *Feel an eye.* Hill,
throttle. Slope, coast. Sky breaks—curbside. I see tire-marked roadkill.
Light splashes on my windshield. Papers, proof, plates; we good. Grass has
crunch. *nah-nah.* Boots on gravel. I'm in uniform, no name tag—*If I lose
the polo, would I look more residential?*   Slide window.   The ray

snares me white. I swallow a tooth and yield my daddy's name:
papers, proof, plates.   *This my daddy's car, we good?*

August stains my collar, the judge gavels;   three months to feel freedom.

87 regular. Twenty on three. Don't need full, last me this week. Squeeze each ounce, clang spout. Petroleum won't combust outside its tank. Got somewhere to be. *nah-nah*, gotta be.

TRAPHOUSE

In the House

Welcome to the most dreaded edifice of the living realm
where haunts whelm flesh into gastric muck and vultures
slurp the gutsy gunk. *Watch your step.* Electric-blue
goop seeps from floorboard rot, claw thrusts from hiding-
place of hawk's throat, widow with gossamer veil chews—

Her bloody fingers, dolls siphon souls from luckless folks.
Cling to walls. Jet bats nip cutlets neck to ankle, hordes
of beetles fester from cancerous ghouls' canker sores,
half-torso of burned-to-life arsonist flares from master's trunk,
100 kilo silkworm cocoons taxidermist's moose. *Open this door.*

Pupils anticipate in cracks, algae-hued fog shrouds amphibian
minions, veilspawn mastiffs drool mercury bile, drywall nails
spell names of unfortunates slain. *Say a word.* Ghastly portraits
whisper mandates to possessed household fixtures: chandelier
sob to sleep, Persian rug froth pregnant leeches, furnace crackle

Deadmister's shadow. *Fight.* Bonedust butcher hacks
swaying livestock—meat medley, sewerstank mechanic
rouses chainsaw to song, white pajamas-child drags
animated couch-sized werecub. *Escape.* Become outcasts:
flaps of muscle gunning past our range. Out there,

Anything can touch.

Oh brother, where did all the bullets go

I ask of it patience, tonight, this gun one militia
propped against sheetrock, my brother's reach
maybe just this evening, afraid all day. His heart
is splitting slowly as is his mind most mornings.
Seems it jumps, trembles sweat, thick secretions
(trouble, secrets) its mushed earth gushes crude
machines tug.

*

My brother practices *lock cover watch*. His guise: shutter plastic, plexiglass.
Into this gun, once (often twice) nightly, a clip of copper-iron fat maggots
slide-sinks in this gun's want. A bit sticks out; he palm-pats its bottom fit
almost how he burps his newborn daughter before lights out. He raises this
soot-camouflaged gun toward storm door, ceiling-floor-window, swings to
and from: a wind vane monitoring whether to ward this direction or that
one. His forehead vein: close rupture, closer splatter. He levers safety white-
red, this gun and him breathes, glides his fingers to its trigger. I think-hear,
"empty the maggots," see them spewing as pulsed light.

*

My brother is servant to none yet unsure what governs him. Is it instinct
for him at the sign of "the end of times" to ground himself in lines that
wind hours, blocks into gunner's knot to shop arms? He loops, "these are
the end of times, the end of days." He's not saying having a piece makes
him safe. He's showing me how he, if brinked, may flare the land with
rattle & metal to protect its darkest inhabitants. I want to say, *that's radical*
to the *necessary* he carries in gaze. All this unsaid revolves us, two brothers,
his living room which despite having lived here for three years holds only
table, salvaged chairs.

*

In peripheral, on table, a torn-open ammo box repurposed
napkin holder. I should ignore it, it ignores me. All this time
in his company, his demonstration, our brotherly banter
spliced with his dread ". . . the end of times, the end of days."
I can't shake its acclimation, his tabletop decor. *Oh brother,*
where did all the bullets go? I'm unsure if it's in me
to see the holes.

Anotha Brotha

shoves away gun
forbids clenched fist
lifts fingertips
rams them against

my skull. Dull as the least-loved toy
my head. Hypermagnetized compass
my face. Display window smudged

with the grease of his touch.
He pushes my nose up, I try
to snuff air. The white collar gnaws
my Adam's apple. A buzzing beaver bound
in his grip nips away my widow's peak,
digs dam from temple to temple.

I pray *escape*,
Leroy swivels his neck into
"please don't mess up this time" look.
The brotha behind us shrugs,
"The youngin' has to learn someday."

Does it need to be
on my crown:
for trimmers to rake its teeth
against my scalp,
for palms to make basketball
of my jaw?

I ask him, "What's the damage?"
He tells me, "14."
Which brings me back to—

Red Delicious cheek
blackberry-bushed mouth
alleyway gravel cutting
head and shoulders
fourteen-year-old me staring
at revolver—anotha brotha
that almost killed me.

Would

Play Maxo Kream's "Meet Again"

Bleach nah, Pine-Sol suffice.
Splinter scent citrus splay-
spray clean. Maplewood,
Rosewood, Parkwood,
great land.

Trail of sol imbue
shadowboxing must, double
dutch gravel powder, loud stank—
folk would draw to subdue funk
making inside, outside throb.

Fo'teen, know little
about *12 Angry Men.*
Less 'bout twelve boys.

Grayland.
They rock Fo'teen,
steal jaw, pinecone takes skull.
Clothesline brobro curl like Dorito
bodyslam six-speed, stamp Jumpman
rip brobro paper-mache.

Fo'teen don't know no names.
Aint saying nothing.

Cuzo's mouth shoots
cuz fists droop, things poppin'.
Cuz watch six of them
come out the cut. Fo'teen,

brobro—bullet—six of them
catch up. Fo'teen look straight at sun.
Sol belch brilliance on everyone.
Them bolts: knuckle, heel—
beam a being, breathing.
Fo'teen a bright child.
Don't got words for nobody.

Graylin.
Nobody, nobody knows
sprays Graylin. Fo'teen
won't speak 'bout nobody's dirt.
Grime, scum, pests
Pine-Sol takes all.

When a Tree Falls

When a tree falls in Richmond a cloud swept down
forms puddles and fog dense enough to entomb.

Most of our city hears it, even if a rock concert of cicadas crash
their tymbals turned cymbals clash a clamorous end.

When a tree falls in Richmond half of our city's grandmas
dust off kerosene lamps, quarter of mamas light
Family Dollar candles, while all young folks jar
fireflies in their camera phone's eye.

Somebody hand me lighter
for when a tree falls in Richmond it's the first time
that tree is shown in the news, our mayor gives a speech
he aint prepared to speak—

Somebody's child goes missing.
Their school desk is packed with art projects,
math take-home tests—tell me
who would dare to clear its contents?

A tree falls in Richmond, you realize that all of this
once was forest; if you knew the difference between:

dogwood, sugar maple, black gum, sourwood,
yellow poplar, river birch, Virginia pine,
pignut hickory, and post oak trees, wouldn't
you remember their names?

After April 11, 2021
for Daunte Wright

Before gun goes off, swear I won't run.
      There's no bullet with my name on it,
I have no name. Have heat, warm liquid
      sloshing basin-body. Taser's teeth
matter me hot kettle. Never favored metal,
      not even in toys played when little. By living
shrapnel caulks up morsels, cracks I cannot
      conceal: molar amalgam, digit graphite, handbled
razor—say *warrant*, show warring, say *taser*
      show holstered pistol, say *taser* show blared barrel—

Say I did run, wouldn't that excuse gun?

Witness

I wasn't there yet I was there
        I didn't feel pain, I did feel pain
what I saw was, I didn't see
        tell me stranger, ask again
how can cannot this be

If I say anything I'll be afraid
        I'll be afraid if I don't speak
there's got to be end to this
        if I look away
I lose everything, I lost everything.

The footage is only few minutes
        it drags few hundred feet in me
each time I click *play*, a life
        is reduced menace
what was, or will its color be?

Isn't burgundy brutal pigment
        so much blue blushed red
a plum drained prune
        a bruised cheek, flushed chest
drenched matter brightens it.

Blicky

Chopping districts
Into sticks
      Blaring wards
      Into boards
You see B
      Bet not blink
Good as gone
        Quick so quit
Blicky shredded-body
      Look like somebodies
B wouldn't rob ya
      Accomplice no problem

No safety swinging
      Toting round &
             Round
People pitted fruit
      Steal lives town–
             town   //

Through day, dawn and dusk
Blicky see a # of things

Errybody who's missing
Everybody who misses

      Saw dey partner on a shirt
Now erryday Blicky chokes

No <u>console</u>   glove compartment
No safe kitchen cabinet

Blicky can't get no <u>sleep</u>
Sees neighbors laid to rest

Blicky tries therapy
Tho as B speaks dey <u>sing</u>

Cross of elegy and pop
It's a hit with <u>erryone</u>

wat dey do

dey suspeck
only house on dis block
got three, fo' vehicles
parked up front

always got dey lights on
early up, late burn
twenty-fo seven guess
come 'n' go

dust 'n' wet wit ink bet—
dey stacks-on-stacks
slim envelopes cash
dey mean business

labor on holidays
function, maybe, nah-nah
talk 'bout dey dead-lines
stay tellin' stories

done heard 'bout ridahs blah
dey wellness check
overdue, watch wat dey do
poepoe come thru

Bando Ballade

Play Migos's "Bando"

Brobro aint no shootah fool
Ridah got da glizzy on him
Leave scum leakin' chicken stool
Talk about root vegetables. When
Goons and ghouls get-to bustin'
Dem boys suited lethal homie
Dey holla, *Free my cousin*—
Who gon hear dey testimony?

Brotha stoop squat, janky mule
Sling sockrock, pass slime to slim
Dey can't trust dis son wit no tool
Aint no clue who brotha might dim.
Done seen slugs glaze hot sauce on rim
Droppin' Sugar Ray like 'Don Lee
Mishap steel, spew putty and phlegm
Who gone? Him here, dat's de money!

Youngboy snapback front fiendish gruel
Don Julio bawls down bottom
Don't talk 'bout dis business—gag rule
Crown Vics creep and snatch night cotton.
Lost kin flash-ash burnah may hymn
Migos meatloaf *hors dirge* groaning
Slobber words judicial bedlam
Oow gawd, hear detested moaning.

         *

Brothers stolen out in the open
Pinned men given slop, bologna
Court appointed plea deal lynchin'
Hooligans; adhere this moment.

Grey Gah

Brotha got passport; *we worldly now.* Dem clouds hoggin' heaven, brotha chillin' window seat exit row. 'Magine scopin' city glitz, smokestacks, cornfields—bet dey fit in brotha's pinch whole plane squint dis new-new getup. Brotha make economy lavish, hollah highyah brotha made somethin' of—*'skews me? What you mean this not my seat?*

    Turbines siphon raspy blue: from long haul, force dull chortle

Preflight thought of falling: alar limbs failing, remnant flesh whisk-yolk, wind thicken vapor welts plaid on body. Clear sky aside few clouds *grey, dull* watercolor (close matter) can't distinguish plunge from drown, air inundates tuba of me, plays one-lung long note, goes—

    Hasting through slow drizzle, swift hiss stuns all daring to rush

Don't trust no plane, don't trust no winged thing, see no comfort suspended midair, neck gets crook just thinking 'bout that angle. High up, ears pop, muddle talk—don't got no business unconscious, take chance on rails, not them kingdom come entrails. Body only a body inside some thing. Reduced hands and feet, climb or crawl before takeoff. *Grey gawd.* Hovering soul dissolves to wisp, body simmers to whisper. Become undone legend, leas' someone's prayer.

Notes on Kumite

Zero   ○

Karate   the merger of
Kara 空   meaning empty
Te 手   meaning hand—

> you are sky
> which means
> you are bare
> unarmed yet
> unalarmed by
> vulnerability
> show me with
> your eyes how
> your hands
> will act.

Ichi   一

From anyone's gaze
your foe should be as you are
in hall that expands
as each of you breathe
on opposite ends, distance is set
breath's length   only their gaze
and your focus can compress
this space.

Ni   二

Opponent is partner.
There is rhythm not music don't think—
if this was dance there would only be
grace.   Grace has no voice
in the absence of self   and other.

San   三

Let go of yourself to obtain yourself.

Yon   四

This is supposed to be agonizing
            let it be.
there is peace   somewhere;   it will not show itself
If you ask . . .   are you aware

            of what you are *in?*

Go   五

Sensei says,

                    they take skin, you take flesh
                    they take flesh, you take bone
                    they take bone, you take life.

Roku 六

To find an opening   you must
         be open
            attack as you block—
         don't ever block
            there is no defense—
    no reason to attack

         you're in sequence

            compliance is not acceptance

Payback Gets Played Back

after James Brown

Youngboy don't know karate,
not even shape of his own fists.

He gloves Timberland sole with jawbone–
swole lip. He's full of salt, gravel, chunks
of asphalt; he retches rocks polished
reddish bile, snot.

For chicken change, they arrange him: falsetto.
Gold batted against his diamond, got him
pitching midnight out they ghetto.
Don't have any honey? They'll settle—

mud. Drag him through trenches slummed
by chumps, who call him bruh yet deny their filth.

*

Lord, lord youngboy drop ka-razor copped da gun
Lord, lord ol boy holla a hollow for everyone
  Lawd, Lawd,   Get back! Da brotha comin'!
        Oh naw   Them trees fall
                  Keep running—
                            Get DOWN

No ka-razor, keen more on shape of fist
as it napkins philtrum back in nose's bridge.
Youngboy wants revenge yet his method caws
a murder of mothers to question their god
what lord creation desecrates own brood?

*

Lying there beside him, the old him:
                        honey-catacombed
                        bubbling in his fructose
                        tar beneath spitting him up
                                    bit by bit
            didn't notice—
his mad, mad collection plate mouth
                        cussin' up metal
smelts together:
lightning rod
Youngboy don't pray to no god,
                        oh lord witness
Otherworldly light, those who near
will know his name.

Acquisition: Coded Language Scroll

Hold conduit. Drum woven past unravel rhapsody
how we cane–be? Summon precursor seer
heard self utter tactile rhythm; rub soles, corral
heartz' frequency, pinch with pitch—we chorus
hostage-*unseen*. Synthetic beings confute reel
home theater display this splay: coagulate state

Hydrogen removed, crude spoil. Colorless rasp
hiss self black-continent, throbstrum dim strata
hijacked ore extract matter, residual chemicals
hinder we. Digitized enterprise music channel
handsome rantsome: generations' clips, remixed
hunted albums, outcome's slathered soundless

Heir self, inhale. Feint rattle: percussive contagion
hem brass-wood, gear tar-organ, cordless speaker
Hear, language seize profit end clews, waves revue

Ah-man

Across landlocked plains sky chase land, fades cornflower blue gristle
of imperceptible distance. Haven't seen dawn chew blue like this since
Pacific spat magenta on Hermosa shore. Sand slurred costal calm's fizzing
touch; toes fuss soles recollecting merger with Virginia Bay. Solvent
body, solution inside reactive to what's outside me. Iron-dense dim hold
captives, kin—cargo hidden where sol won't trail. Fail at dissolving, can't
join Atlantic's burden. Bereaved won't make space. They pray, *Build
your house above sea, amen.* Encountered land with thirst for me. Taking
belongings, long for familiar—some strong sense of place—knot in this
continent gnawing its residents, bound literature, law, scripture of God—
Father who guided forefathers to prosper with iron and hemp, loosen my
ties to land. Tides remind *the passage* is no man's fissure to seal. Inundated
with blues, sail, fill hue-mid.

> Dawn to dusk,
> sun dries meat of mollusks
> waves scavenge what remains

Vessel, soon you'll be assembled. Here is your hull bark from magnolia's
earlier saw. Didn't think to fetch hammer, clamor you whole with skull.
There go my nails, dripping loss perhaps my mess works adhesive? Steady,
the deck's almost built. Lug parcels of rail tracks, shake off clung earth,
bind with rope and lay in rows neat and snug. Raise mast to filth solar
observance with shadow. Welt ladder along its pelt, string sewn sails made
from bleached battle flags wor-ship width. *Ah man*, forgot material for my
cabin. Ray things going, find peace under whatever bit of matter is leftover.

> Atop the crow's nest:
> against light-swamped sky
> blues rich as flesh

Drift endless, wind drag me an end. Bottom upturn divulge *our fall*. Can't escape tethered, sunken place, surface. *Whale omen, gurawn, gurawn, gurawngurawn gurawn*—sink holy, ground deliver. Homecoming, it's been so long.

    dim wreckage
    a shark wouldn't bite—
    go on sol, nothing's here.

Brotha Moves

(palinode I hoped wouldn't be)

—it's in me to see the holes. Another Black life—stolen. I'm told I
shouldn't be ~~unruly~~? I think it's time I grade my hands a nine; get familiar
with this caliber. Join the Black militia fending Blue officials. I don't think
they get me. I grew up Cap City. Nah, aint never held gun, not even toy
resembling one. Feared spray, nozzle erases everything considered blight.
I'm inclined to revisit the Second Amendment, make amends for my
dimmed kin looking from the soil-heaven they've been placed in. What
good were the 10s I spent self-defensing, kumite, karate—empty fist
nonsensing if some vigilante or bandit with badge decides to brass-tag
me or anotha? Nah-nah, my brothers-in-arms are on something *right*.
They ready, trust me, we ready. We don't accept this stand your ground
stagnation, who's really believing it's gonna get better? *Colorblind progress*
... shoo thinking they progressive cause they read *New Jim Crow*, talking
'bout how they copped that Ta-Nehisi Coates, watch 'em name dropping
Martin, Malcolm, spend half the day reciting Morrison and Baldwin
quotes. What damned world is resting after three *trained* officers barge
Louisville home at dontdisturbmypeace hours of night and volleys rounds
in house, at our kin Breonna Taylor? What damned world is idle as one
trained-*veteran*-officer during rush hour daylight drops knee on the neck
of our kin George Floyd? Dem boys in blue, goddamn, goddamn I am not
a person of rage (but these days, my people). These days, I wonder how in
these wonderbread counties I've vagabon'd through I haven't snapped like
the summer stung cornstalks I imagine could bury me standing. Err-time
an officer or civilian-with-gun's around, I tense up, switch my whole, tidy
demeanor. Programming got me disrupted—I'm supposed to function?
Prosper? How ye? How ye? They talk self-care, take a mental health day.
Nigga, I need a mental health year my nigga. I need more than some
$600 dollar get-by. Nah, I'm not grateful. Too many lives G, too many
lives. I'm shook—poem don't got no line breaks—I'm afraid of the line,
won't talk out of line, walk out line, don't want no flat lines—Don't get me

started lineage. This reparations-ish, nobody really knows how to make it work, without paying back *the work*. There are college campuses, size plantations. Figure out how to reverse-repair-retribute over 250 years of slavery, mangled culture, history, hundreds of images distorting self-worth, disparities in health, economics, housing, education—figure out those numbers and don't have 'em write a check. Nah, write me and mines the inheritance they believed belonged to American sons and daughters. I'm not a revolutionary. I (just) don't want to die. I got some stuff of poems talking 'bout "When I go" and ish. Know this; see me. Don't have holes in me yet and not trying to. But yo, a nigga got spirits and get live with ghosts. If it takes me toting anotha arm to halt somebody from ensuing harm on me and mines, let me see 'bout this iron. I'm from mud. Maggots lurched and I danced with them. I tongued dirt and laughed. I know gutta from sewer—know grime, grit, and can spit slime that'll melt guts to sap. Not errybody street, not errybody woke. But errybody can tell which choppa or burnah made them trees fall. I say this (and this in confidence), that I'm not trying to be one seen on dark-mode dusked screens. Yo what Tupac say? I aint one to push but if pushed, watch how far I go

When I go

it will be brilliant day
with sun that blurts soul,
extinguishes dim.
The houses, vehicles,
nothing of them will escape.

I'll step onto block
rocking Jordans somebody
would kill for. I'll bare hairy legs,
shorts hardly reaching
my lopsided knees.

White tee gown me,
otherworldly bright.

Hair trimmed at No. 2
taper fade at No. 0.
I'd watched YouTube the night befo'
learn the cutting technique
my daddy never showed.

I'll keep my widow's peak,
slim-slim my sideburns.

Stride off that side, foot the road.
Crease my sneaks some growing crow's-feet
keep walking through soulless solar.
The perplexed will shuttercrack gander,
Who dis fool steppin' out dere like dey own de day?

I'll take it in. Arms dangle,
trunk sways. Cleave my face
molar-molar gleaming.
I'll stop, crouch at violet
sprouted where curb hits asphalt.

Just sitting there, tending itself,
not worried 'bout nothing.

NOTES

The book epigraph comes from a magazine interview with the late blues pianist, singer, and songwriter Eddie Boyd. See "'Nobody Makes Me Crawl' Part 2," *Blues Unlimited*, no. 88 (January 1972), 11.

The part title "House below the Heavens" is an homage to the hip-hop album *Below the Heavens*, by Blu & Exile.

"IEP" stands for Individual Education Plan, a legal document that outlines the learning program for children who meet the criteria for at least one of the thirteen eligibility categories identified by the Individuals with Disabilities Education Act of 2004 (IDEA). A problem I would like to note is that often school administrators and evaluators aren't trained to be culturally aware or responsive to the needs and experiences of youth of color. Ultimately, this leads to the misdiagnosis of and inadequate support for youth of color. By contrast, Lupe Fiasco's song "Paris, Tokyo" offers the speaker a glimpse of the limitless freedom that may be accessible to him based on his education plan.

"Acquisition: Mothership" is a tribute to the P-Funk Mothership that appeared during the 1970s music group Parliament-Funkadelic's song "Mothership Connection." The band's leader, George Clinton, would emerge from the landed Mothership after it was summoned during the performance of the song. The Mothership is currently on display in the Musical Crossroads exhibit at the Smithsonian National Museum of African American History and Culture.

"Acquisition: Boombox Carried by Radio Raheem" is a tribute to fictional character Radio Raheem, played by the late actor Bill Nunn in Spike Lee's film *Do the Right Thing* (1989). Several additional characters from the film are referenced, including Da Mayor, Buggin' Out, and Mother Sister. The Boombox is currently on display in the Musical Crossroads exhibit at the Smithsonian National Museum of African American History and Culture.

"Cop a" is in conversation with hip-hop artist Nas's song "Got Ur Self A Gun" released on his 2001 album, *Stillmatic*. The poem is written in the twenty-three-line "bop" form, which was invented by Afaa Michael Weaver during a Cave Canem poetry retreat.

"His Bounty" references the song "Ruff Ryders' Anthem" by late hip-hop artist DMX, and "Heaven Sent" by R&B singer Keyshia Cole.

"Acquisition: Coltrane's Saxophone" is the product of (1) a conversation I had in 2019 with a Smithsonian Museum curator and researcher about one of John Coltrane's saxophones, and (2) my listening to Coltrane's previously unreleased album from 1964, *Blue World* (2019).

"Acquisition: Dress from *Lady Sings the Blues*" is a tribute both to Billie Holiday and to Diana Ross, who played Holiday in the 1972 film *Lady Sings the Blues*. The lynchings of Jesse Washington (Waco, Texas, 1916) and Emmett Till (Mississippi, 1955) are referenced in the poem. Additionally, this poem alludes to "Strange Fruit," one of the songs for which Holiday is most known. The dress from *Lady Sings the Blues* is in the collection of the Smithsonian National Museum of African American History and Culture.

"Snowfall with Ruth Brown's *Bringdown*" is in conversation with the song "Rain Is a Bringdown," by the late singer and "Queen of R&B" Ruth Brown. While doing archival research at the Smithsonian, I found letters between Ruth Brown and Jonas Bernholm, a Swedish record producer known for reissuing jazz, blues, and R&B music. Bernholm reissued some of Ruth Brown's music through his record company Route 66 in the early

1980s. For more about their relationship and work see the Jonas Bernholm Rhythm and Blues Collection, 1976–1991, Archives Center, National Museum of American History.

"Day, Dawn & Dusk Mess with My Blues" is a tribute to the 1940s musical trio Day, Dawn & Dusk. The original members were Bob Carver (Day), Eddie Coleman (Dawn), and Gus Simons (Dusk). Their musical style varied from spirituals to swing. They could sing in four different languages, toured throughout Europe, and even recorded several soundies (1940s low-budget music films played from a Panoram). They were also known for their comedic renditions of operettas, including *Faust* and *Rigoletto*. I originally read through newspaper clippings about their performances at the Smithsonian. See the Bernice Johnson Reagon Collection of The African American Sacred Music Tradition, Circa 1822–1994, Archives Center, National Museum of American History.

"4:04 A.M." puts Day, Dawn & Dusk in sync with Atlanta-based trap group Migos, featuring artists Quavo, Offset, and the late rapper Takeoff. This poem is written as a tribute to Takeoff.

"Apple Pie" references the history of the Pullman Company and Pullman porters. Following the Civil War, the Pullman Company hired formerly enslaved African American men and women as porters (sleeping car attendants) and maids to serve on the Pullman sleeping and dining cars. Many of the African American men who worked as sleeping car attendants were called "George" by the white patrons aboard, as if they were the property of George Pullman, the company founder.

"After April 11, 2021" is an elegy for twenty-year-old Daunte White, who was killed by officer Kimberly Porter during a traffic stop in Brooklyn Center, Minnesota. There is footage and documentation of the murder widely available, so I will not go into detail. Though I will note that Officer Porter threatened to tase White and yelled, "Taser, Taser, Taser!" Thereafter she shot him with her pistol.

"Blicky" is slang for a gun, most commonly a pistol. Not to be confused with "glizzy," which specifically refers to a glock. The underlined words, read consecutively in order, constitute an envoi.

"Acquisition: Coded Language Scroll" is a tribute to Saul Williams and his impact on poetry and literary and performance arts. The Coded Language Scroll, a prop Williams used in performances of the poem "Coded Language," is in the collection of the Smithsonian National Museum of African American History and Culture.

"Brotha Moves": We won't forget 2020.

ACKNOWLEDGMENTS

Many thanks to the editorial staff of the following journals and anthologies in which these poems—sometimes in previous forms—first appeared. *The Bennington Review*: "Sugar"; *Black Warrior Review*: "Brotha Speaks"; *Blood Orange Review*: "Sunday before Last"; *A Garden of Black Joy: Global Poetry from the Edges of Liberation and Living*: "Of the White Tee"; *Interim*: "Nah-Nah: Trap Haibun," "Notes on Kumite"; *Juke Joint Magazine*: "A Drive through July Showers"; *Obsidian*: "Anotha Brotha," "Apple Pie"; *The Racket Journal*: "Cut the Grass," "Hustle Hard," "Yesterday"; *Revolute*: "Nine Mile Road."; *Stonecoast Review*: "Bando Ballade"; *The Southern Poetry Anthology, Volume IX: Virginia*: "Ah Bae: Blues Haibun," "When a Tree Falls"; *Witness*: "Payback Gets Played Back."

My sincere gratitude to the editorial team at Northwestern University Press for believing in this work. It is an honor and great joy to have my debut collection find a home at Curbstone Books.

This work would not be possible without generous support and funding from the Smithsonian, University of Iowa Writers' Workshop, and the Fine Arts Work Center in Provincetown.

At the Smithsonian, I would like to first thank my research advisers Dr. Nancy Bercaw of the National Museum of American History (NMAH) and Dr. Kevin Strait of the National Museum of African American History and Culture for their guidance and support of my work during my 2019 Summer Graduate Student Fellowship at the NMAH. I also want to thank Dr. John Troutman for our delightful conversations about museum curation and music.

Many thanks to the University of Iowa African American Studies program, specifically my advisor Dr. Richard B. Turner for his indispensable support, mentorship, and encouragement.

I want to thank the Iowa Writers' Workshop community, particularly my professors in poetry Mark Levine, Elizabeth Willis, James Galvin, and Tracie Morris. I also want to thank Connie Brothers, Lan Samantha Chang, Sasha Khmelnik, Jan Zenisek, and Deb West for their support.

To my fellow Iowa poets, especially Amanda Auerbach, Joseph Duffy, Abby Ryder-Huth, Gwen Muren, and Lucy Dunphy Barsness, thank you all for your early readership of these poems.

I'm deeply grateful for my poetry mentors, Aracelis Girmay, John Murillo, Heather Madden, Djola Branner, Kyle Dargan, and Joel Dias-Porter. Thank you for your guidance, care, and unyielding support.

Dear Family, Tameka Cage Conley, 'Gbenga Adeoba, Claretta Holsey, Angela Tharpe, Esther Ifesinachi Okonkwo, Elaine Ray, Kenneth Ibegwam, Michaeljulius Idani, Romeo Oriogun, Joseph Emanuel, Janelle Effiwatt, Joshua Leonard, Alonzo Vereen, Matthew B. Kelley, Arinze Ifeakandu, Kofi Opam, Tiffany Tucker, Darius Stewart, Lisa Covington, Indya Finch, Alexia Arthurs, Marlene Effiwatt, Shaquille Brissett, Afabwaje and Philip Kurian—thank you for always holding me down, love y'all. And to Siyanda Mohutsiwa, you've always been my number one.

Dearest Friends, Inés Rodriguez, Azia Armstead, and Alexis K. Reed— where would I be without your love? Love y'all dearly. Crystal, Nick, Jasmine, Erick, Allison, Max, Julia, Viktor, Paris, Vadon, Baleja, and Kite, y'all have my love. For saving this manuscript from mediocrity: Meagan Washington, you have my deepest gratitude and love. For listening to me ramble about music and so much more: thank you dearly, Yuuka. And to my partner Fig, ten years counting or ten years remaining? Joking! I love you more each day.

For the Watkins family, Browns, Turners—all my people in Richmond, I'm here for you. I hope you see yourself in me as I see myself in you.

Lastly, to Jody, Colbey, and Malachai, I love y'all with my everything, and y'all are everything.